THE GREATNESS IN YOU

A seed within you

Busiswa Singama

Busiswa Singama

The greatness in you- A seed within you
Published by

© 2019 Busiswa Singama
First impression 2019

ISBN: 978 0 620- 85982-0

Cover and book designed by Mbana Publishing and Printing

Printed in South Africa by Mbana Publishing and Printing

AN EVERYDAY DECLARATION

I am the head
I am above
I am strong
I am smart
I am a positive influence
I am successful in my career.
I am loved
I am a new creation
I am a wonderful person
I am an achiever
I am beautiful/ handsome
I am born for greatness
I am a living testimony
I am blessed above measures
I am healthy
I am prosperous
I own my space
I am what God says I am
I am the Body of God

AMEN

Acknowledgement

First of the most, I would love to thank God for the gift of life and wisdom that He has entrusted me with. I thank Him for using me as a vessel to change and heal the nation of this generation. He has created everyone for a better life and to live our lives with passion and fullness.

I would love to thank my mother and sisters for supporting and encouraging me in everything I am doing. Thanking them for praying with me. Thank you family for your love you have been giving me from the day one of this writing experience. I have the ability to change people's lives for all of this, I thank my family for trusting and mostly believing in me.

I thank every idea and everyone who is involved in this book. My words cannot express the love and appreciation towards you guys.

I acknowledge my friends and fans who believes in my motivations and my quotes when I send them through their phones. Your pushing me to write every day has led me to release a book, your testimonies has kept me going all the time.

The greatness in you- A seed within you

I will never forget to thank my spiritual parents, pastor Nomhle and David-Dee Bhungane for grooming me spiritually and mentor me in all aspects oflife. Your prayers has impacted only the greatness in my life. They would sit with me and share everything good and inspiring and I am grateful for that, they never judge my motives, they always support what I do.

Not forgetting my church mates from I Am church, they are always the best. To everyone contributed in this book. I am grateful and I love you guys.

Amen

Busiswa Singama
2019

Contents

I
Talented soul

It may not always a case for someone to find their talent in their youngest age such as when you are born and discover what you can do but even if you discover your talent at your 40's it's still a given talent. We sometimes tend to believe that we are nothing, useless, worthless because of what people think of us and how we were being treated by our parents sometimes, but the truth is we are not of anyone but God's pupils. When you are at God's best sight, He goes all out to prove that He loves you no matter what, it goes the same to you when you have something you are blessed with. No matter how long it takes to show, but it will eventually do happen because it is meant to be yours. You can also be multi-talented having talents that you know and others that are not yet revealed.

I was around 11-12 years when I noticed my talent in singing. I started singing in high school when I was singing in a school, church and community choir. But as I was growing up I met up some people who helped me to mingle with relevant people to help me pursuing it because as much as I knew about my talent I couldn't go further without people by my side. And even so it was not easy to make it through because of some challenges, my first challenge was the environment. I am from a rural area and I was not exposed to right doors when I can be given an opportunity, challenge two was how and where can I get money to start this singing career, those were two major problems that I had at that time. But because I knew that, that is what I wanted to do I will keep on pushing and take every chance that linked me to what I wanted. As I said earlier that you can be multi-talented, I am also a motivating activist I write motivational books and do motivational talks. That also started long time ago but did not come up very easily, I struggled. I couldn't do my talks because I didn't have a platform to start but since IAM a believer of God I knew something eventually will come. God promised me in His word that He makes a way where it seems to be no way then I kept His word everytime.

You are a soul filled with many talents, bunch of gifts all you need to do is to take the first step and pursue what you believe in. Sometimes living a normal life can get you nowhere. What do I mean by "normal life' I say you cannot sleep over hours, spend much quality time with friends, social media at the same time you want to progress in life. One has to come after another. We want things to come to us but we are lazy to go and find them. There is a phrase saying *"Uzoyithola kanjan'uhlel'ekoneni"* meaning how are you going to get it while sitting and relaxing. If you want things done and ready you get up and do something. Life is unpredictable, it needs someone to be more handful.

If you can look up to those who have achieved some of the things, they did not come up smooth even their start-ups were not easy at all, they struggled, fallen, failed, cried but they did not give up because of the challenges, they knew what they had set their goals and difficulties are there to strengthen them so they will achieve any way with their falls up along. So giving up is never an option to quit your talent.

I wrote my first motivating book but I never had a chance to publish it because I lacked funds. I gave up from it, it ended up missing but I had it in my mind that a dream of becoming an author one day will be fulfilled. Years passed by without writing again. One of the days I visited my dream and asked myself do I really let this to happen letting my dream vanishing and what kind of a coward that makes me. I decided to write again. It was not because I was hopeless and discouraged but I insisted because I love voicing out my opinions and bringing hope to people, preaching and teaching through writing.

We all have the same ideas but it is up to someone to initiate it, because you may find that someone somewhere have the dream similar to mine but I am the one who got the courage to initiate it. You know exactly what you are good at, please do not give up on that keep on doing your best one day it will be recognised and acknowledged. Maybe you have tried your talent to work out with no luck, all I can say is keep on trying because the dark comes first before light. Your dream is your future, fight for it. God gave you because He trusted you and He will make sure that you succeed, He cannot give you something beyond your power

I have a friend of mine who is an artist, he tried to penetrate within the music industry many times failing. He even thought of starting something else and forget about the music. In times things started to fall in places, everything went back good. He is now a multi award winner, well respected and acknowledged within the industry, he is now making weaves in the country and outside the country because he kept on believing that nothing is impossible and he used what he believed in. Giving up is not an option. We also have to talk about our talents to our friends, family and our mates so that they help us to pull through because there is nothing you can do alone, we all need a helping hand for us to be successful.

If you can look in the book of Habakkuk 2:2 it says "*and the Lord answered me and said, write down the vision, and make it plain upon tablets that whoever sees it may run with it*". This simple means we always need someone else to hear/see what we believe in so that they run with it and make it a success.

Most of the people have their talents but it depends on one to do something about their talents, because not everyone is courageous to do something on their own, so they need people to make it possible. The vision is for the future time, if it seems slow in getting together wait patiently for you will reap perfectly, it will not be delayed. Do not worry about time as long as you know what you want and you believe that it will happen be patient, never undermine what you have. Someone sees a potential in you. Another problem that is killing our talents before they even kick in is pride, let us put our pride aside and humble ourselves before people

2
Greener pastures
(Your success)

Planting a seed it does not take any much time but making sure that it grows very well and healthy. It takes about a month or two to grow and be ready to be eaten, in that processing time you wait patiently hoping to get beautiful results at the end. Same goes to your greener pastures (success) it seems to take time and ages but you are assured that it is coming into a right direction, awaiting to blossom and surprise people with juicy results.

I know sometimes we fail to understand that when it is your time to shine, you first meet the darkness, be challenged and go through some deep valleys but at your perseverance something amazing awaits for you. We grow up from different backgrounds and experience different perspectives of life, but our parents taught us one of many things in life * RESPECT*. You can go nowhere if you do not have respect for people. Success is a two way street, it goes with respect and love. If you do not love people and respect them in their positions then you have nothing to offer to the world.

I call it greener pastures because that is where you get your fruits, enjoying your sweating peacefully. No one will question your actions and abilities and no one will fight your ins-outs. You will be entitled to your own greener pastures (*Amadlel'aluhlaza*).

The idea is to encourage you to keep on pushing and striving for what's best. Have faith in what you believe in no matter how small it may look, treasure it and make it worth and stop doubting your power and your strength. Your future is in your mind, initiate it with your hands. In every journey we embark on, we meet challenges and difficulties.

I was once a victim in my teenage stage I found myself in a situation where I thought I will never be able to pursue my dreams again. I was in my matric year in Cape Town where I found myself on a forced marriage (*ukuthwalwa*), I was so confused and disturbed at that time as my year was very busy with a lot of work to be done. I was so miserable not knowing what to do but I managed to escape after I matriculated I left Cape Town for couple of years out of fear and low self-esteem I then saw myself with no passion and no direction. It took me a long time to actually get back to myself and put everything happened behind. I rebuild myself, focusing on my future because time waits for no one. Since then I had never stood low and I continued chasing after my dreams till today I am still heading towards my life. Time wasted never returns, you just need to mend your heart and push even more harder because there is a lot that needs to be done by you. The day I left Cape town I told myself to hate it but then I remembered hatred may lead you to death so I decided to forgive and love myself again. I knew that I have a dream that one day I want to achieve and that day has come. Feeling sorry for what happened is just a waste of time, is not over, dream again and start to live your purpose. A self-driven person can go far than a peer-pressured person. Stay Focused.

Again what kept me going is that I got born again(saved) some years back then my intellectual operation changed, how I speak changed, now I think more of good things than bad. That also changed how I see things from previously, I am more in positive attitude that is why I see that there is nothing impossible when you focus on it. My mind is transformed only because of the word of God that I am studying and some books for encouraging myself.

A good thinker with positive attitude produces better achievements. A success can be defined in many ways but I define it ' as a perfect planning and efforts demonstrated in action'. We all do things differently in planning but the mission is one to succeed. After all that I have encountered in my life, I have surrounded myself with people who have the same vision and mission as mine, I have learnt to think and always stay positive. I shared my space with those in high places in order to improve and achieve more in life. You cannot spend your most time with fishers while you want to be a musician that doesn't make it right, associate your self with people who are already in the field you want to be in. You must be with people whom you sharing your best interests with, try to change your peers, then you will see the direction in your life. They used to say where there is a smoke there is fire, so do I say where there are your vision-careers, there is your success.

The word success is defined as getting something you wanted or intended. When you doing something obviously your intentions is to succeed, that is why we all ought to finish we have started.

In life sometimes we go in different ways, experiencing different pains, proving ourselves to different people for different wrong reasons but we must never get tired on believing in ourselves and trust in our dreams because life can be tricky it needs you to be wiser. When we look at those who have made it up there it looks sweet and honey because they are enjoying every drop of their sweat, yes it is sweet but it doesn't look as honey as it looks. You have to sacrifice lot of your precious time, time with friends, sometimes have your sleepless nights. You lose friends through the process especial those who knows nothing about your vision but you gain points to your success.

There is a verse on Psalms 23 that says, "*the Lord is my Shepherd, whom shall I fear He leadth me into green pastures.*" I love this verse because it talks about being led unto greener pastures, no one can reach those pastures without a leader. Have a mentor, friend or a family member behind your success. It takes two hands to build something solid and strong.

3
A seed within you

A seed that is not nurtured never grows. A seed that is being taken care of when you feel like you want, it also takes time to bloom even delays it's normal time. A seed cannot be contained for more than it should be, even a rose cannot be without a seed. A seed needs to be kept in a good condition in order for the rose to be beautiful. We are the roses and Jesus is a seed, we cannot bloom on our own without a seed planted. We cannot grow an glow without a good seed. The buyers cannot buy and the sellers cannot sell what is not well prepared. We need to be well groomed to be able to operate well. We are the roses of Christ Jesus, Jesus is grooming the seed within us to produce the fruit that will be tasteful, let us allow Him to nurture us and do us good. We are His product, we are a very expensive seed that at no price it can be bought.

You are a rare seed that not everyone can find it, someone need to go all out to find you, wherever you go make yourself visible, shine yourself and make sure that you brightens your ways. You have something that you are keeping within you, you need to come out of your closet and take what you have in you for the world is waiting for your greatness. You always get inspired by what people are doing which is good but have you asked yourself, how about you change it and be the one who inspire others. You are an inspiration yourself, stop allowing people to determine your path and stop doubting yourself and in what you believe in. God will bless it. No idea is weak and worthless especial when you are praying about it. If you do not believe in what you know, then who do you expect to believe it.

You are the one who knows the seed planted in you and people will only see the fruits coming out from what is planted. As I said before I am a believer and I believe so much in what I have prayed for and act through my faith, so the main weapon to fight anything is PRAYER. People are waiting out there hopeless, desperate and some have lost faith in themselves. So you are the asset that is there to bring hope to those with broken hearts and has lost so much. God did not make any mistake by putting the seed within you so that you stand up and share peace and hope to His people. Your story may change how someone else sees and view things from previous. Your attitude can change someone's actions out there. It does not matter how you say it as long someone is getting a message and their actions changes then you must know you have done your good part.

I made an example of a seed because that is the only thing that is able to grow, glow inside the plant then when it's coming out you only see the beauty of what you have planted. Same goes to you when you have all these ideas no one really sees them but they only see your achievement after what you have been doing behind. No one said there won't be any challenges that you may come across, challenges that will make you doubt your ways and question your abilities but that doesn't mean you should give up because nothing come easy. Only one thing that will keep you walking and striving is FAITH. Your talent can take you out of poverty if you stick and pray for it, only if you know your story and you are ambitious about it.

Put everything down in order as you are planning and let God take His part. God cares for you and loves you very much. You are a seed ready to blossom for people to see what is being kept inside, you are like a bomb that is waiting to blast for a greatness. Be bold and go for what is yours, the world is waiting for your talent. So get up work on it and achieve it.

4
True self never dies

How to determine true love? What different between loyalty and honesty? Have you ever wondered what will happen when everyone else has left with self? To all those questions I only have one answer that says your true self never leaves you nor dies. They used to say if you want loyalty rather buy a dog, it does not have to be like that if you can stay true to yourself. Be true in what you want and no matter what or how people react, just remain true to yourself. All the years I was trying to find myself from other people, I was caught up in what people were saying about me, what people were thinking about me because every time after doing something I would wait for a compliment from people then if they didn't I would feel small, angry, insecure and unhappy and doubt what I have done if it was a good thing to do or not.

I was caught up in that miserable life for quite a few years, saying that when I have done something I need to be congratulated until a random day where I went to visit some old age home in Pretoria without anyone knowing, then on my conversation with other granny she said something about people who do not recognise anything good from others than when it is done by themselves. I did not pay any attention at that moment, but on my way back home I then thought to myself about what the granny said and I told my mind that from now on I must stop listen or wondering what people think or say about me and if it console my soul and I feel good about it then the second person has nothing to say in my life so that is how I decided to stay true to myself and listen to what I feel and want because intro-spection never lies and it will never fool you.

In my language isi Xhosa they say *'ithemba alibulali kodwa liyadanisa '*. Because I remember hoping that I will get a deal in a local radio station in Pretoria and as a woman of God I had faith in it, if it went well then I will be able to spread the word of God through broadcasting. But as time went by things got very bad and I couldn't achieve my desire and I couldn't get what I was hoping to get, that is when I said indeed hope never kills anyone you just get disappointed. I lost faith and hope, then I decided to go back home to Eastern Cape just to relax my mind and think afresh for a while not saying I forgot about my talent and dreams, I was just gaining strength and courage again.

But because I knew my vision and what I wanted, so I went back to self and said yes I am disappointed in people again but what about my true self, am I going to stop all this because of failures I had and I won't have any other idea other than this one. Then I re-visited my writing talent because writing is one of the platform to share your pain, disappointments, worries and motivations then I went back and write those stories. Not saying I quit a broadcasting thing I am also pursuing it because I am true in what I want. Love is a beautiful thing anyone can die to experience, love goes together with respect. If you have love and respect for yourself then nothing can stop what you believe is possible. Love is patient and kind. Love is not proud or rude. Love does not demand it's way. Love keeps no record of wrongs. Love rejoices whenever truth wins out. Love never gives up and it never loses faith. Love is always hopeful, lastly love endures through every circumstances.

There is a part that says love is patient and kind, when you are always on a hurry, you want things to be done immediately then where is patience. Love never gives up but because of one failure or unsuccessful enquiry then you already giving up and done. You must never lose faith on yourself. Love is always hopeful and endures every obstacle, meaning there will always be challenges along the way but when true love is within you, no challenge can beat that. It all starts inside then appears to people as a confident.

Confident starts from your inner being, you cannot be able to express yourself if you are not confident enough and you cannot expect someone else to believe in what you are saying if you are failing to do that yourself. Confident is in the same hand with self-respect, when you respect yourself enough, you care less of what people think of you.

5
Shaped future awaits for no one

They say life begins at the age of 40, but it is up to you to begin your life as soon as you can be able to think of something. The day you are able to make decisions of your own that is the day you must start preparing for your future, time wasted never returns. No one will mould your future except yourself, make good friends, take good decisions and choose your surroundings wisely while you still have time in your hand.

I played with most of my time because no one advices me on a right way in terms of how must I use my time. I did not have that privilege at my youth time, only now that I have been given such advices. But even now they are still relevant and still helpful because I am benefiting from them and I am able to advise others too. Life is a long-range race that everyone is given his/her lane to run on but because we have different lanes we tend to delay on the road but the purpose is one to finish the race, and we have to reach the finishing line so we ought to help each other on the way.

You doing so well in your race until you see someone struggling on the way and you think your race is difficult as that of that person, you just have to be sure of what you are doing and help that person with her along. That is what

I call shaping life together when you do not laugh when you see someone else struggling. I am now proud to say I am a better person because of people I mingled with, they taught me many things in different ways. Things that I have carried taught me that everywhere I go there will always be there in my present and future time but I will conquer with them along because they are there to give me even more strength. You will hear people saying they had good friends but because of life challenges they ended up with bad friends. Some will say they were not thinking straight but because no one was there to offer their hand to be hold, yes there are good friends but not all of them are good enough in supporting and be there in your life

We as black people do not want to help each other, infact we are not there at each other's lives as people of one nation. If you are not my relative then I have nothing to do with what is happening in your life, that is how our mindset works but the truth is we need each other for us to overcome every broken and un-appreciated heart of anyone. Our youth of today is so miserable, we are caught up in our own issues, we are angry at each other in a way that we are not even able to see if someone next to you is going through some storm. We have abandoned each other while we are of the same nation coming from One Creator. People are going through depressions and are caught up in anxiety because they have no one to talk to, and we have no one to ask how are we doing and no one is willing to listen to us. We have missed the point of helping and sharing each other's burdens, we are too busy with our own lives trying to live up the standard and we totally forgot to strengthen and stretch a helping hand.

Unity is about moulding each other at any costs. We really need to stop this and change our attitude and this mindset of stereotyping people. With unity and togetherness we can be able to shape our futures and prosper together. There are change shakers, activists, motivational speakers who are going all out to make sure that they are doing their best in shaping other people and sharing their best of interests to shape their lives for the better, let us co-operate in making our tomorrow more better than today. People are busy streaming themselves for every opportunity they can get to better their future and you are still busy wishing others a bad luck, that is not how life is. You cannot do bad to people and expect things to be smooth for you.

We lack integrity, determination and self love as people because we do not have our time as families and friends, we busy looking at other people's lives. Life is fun and sweet when you are focusing on what is yours. Let us help each other to strengthen up and stirs up our future and hold it through to the end. It all begins within self and goes outside to people. Prepare what you want to see tomorrow today. Shape who you want to see tomorrow in you and make no regrets. It begins with you when you decide to stop making excuses and shift blame to whoever for what you have done wrong.

Shake every dirtiness in you and pull yourself together for the future. I repeat it do not hold grudges of what happened years back, flash everything and begin to mould yourself for a better day to come. Only God knows what do we have in stores for the next day but you can assure your day by at least preparing for it.

When you have life ahead of you, you have a lot to sacrifice first thing is going out everyday with friends spending more time together, depart yourself away from friends with negative attitude and choose friends who have a positive influence in your life and friends who can lead you in good direction. You have so much that you can offer today that might change someone's tomorrow. Be a good example to those who are close to you. Focus on what is right and good. Be concern with what can change your life. Connect yourself with potential people for your better future. Network with relevant and responsible people. Time awaits for no one, only YOU are the one who needs to get things right and focus on achieving them. Prove yourself to anyone rather than being satisfied with your work and what you can do more.

6
Born to rule

We all come from different backgrounds, fighting different battles and have been wounded and we all have faced trials and tribulations. We have been abandoned by people who are special in our lives. We even disappointed at some point. We all have been betrayed by people very close to us and whom we trusted. We all had those moments when we would cry very deeply in our secret places. In one way or another we all have been shaken to a certain extent in our lives, but we get up and rule again. We are born in this cruel world. The world full of evilness always ready to sway and swallow what we have and take our dignity away. We all experience those dull moments where you feel useless, effortless and powerless and you feel like you are crushed. But I say not anymore now you are ready to rule and conquer again.

> You are a warrior
> You are the head and not the tale
> You are smart
> You are genuis
> You are strong
> You are above
> You are wise
> You are a conqueror

You were born with purpose, born with intelligence. Now it is time to rule over, own what is yours and dwell in your purpose and space. You can be knocked down but not out. Falling is something that we know it exists, and it is good to fall first before you get up again so that you may be able to identify your mistakes but the problem starts when you fall and never get up. From all those fall-outs that is where we gain strength and power to get up and do it again and again I have encountered so many breakdowns and knock downs but I told myself not to give up, they were not easy by the time but I told myself to go for what I want, so they just made me to be more strong and open minded.

You are born to prosper, born to rain and rule. You are a product of God who is the Creator of all things. Sometimes you may wonder how and where do I get all of this wisdom and strength to write, well it is not something coming from my own intellectual effect but God the provider is the one who inspired me and deposited every wisdom with the gift I have. It is a great pleasure from above. You are not small and you were created well with brilliant ideas to better up your amazing future with the talent that you have. You are a star, you are a boss of your own and you can shine in whatever you are doing. Just do it with pleasure and a passion.

Do not give up now it is not yet the time for you to give up special not after what you have just started. Remember before climbing to the top you need a ladder for few steps to be on top, yea you need to take few steps in order to be on top. Sometimes you might have this gift or a talent but still seem impossible for you to get on top, listen not everything worth fully comes easy. Remember some orders are taking time to be delivered and I used to say what is big and precious it usually takes time for it to be prepared because it requires lot of time to be done. So in your impatience please remember that powerful things takes time to be delivered. Sometimes it seems impossible to penetrate but push even harder and pray strong.

Success is in your hands, lot of things are placed at your hand but maybe it is not yet time for you to see them. You need to seek them in prayer so that they can be revealed to you clearly. Get up and do something about your life because nothing will come in a tray, it needs you to go out there and be exposed to people with the same vision as yours. NEVER GET TIRED TO HUSTLE FOR WHAT YOU WANT AND REALLY BELIEVES IN.

7
Successful people's mind-set

When you have trained your mind on how to think, then your mind set is changing automatically. Quoting from the book of 2 Kings 4 verse 1-7, *"and Elisha said unto her, what shall I do for thee? Tell me what hast thou in the house? And she said, thine hand maid hath not anything in the house, apart from a pot of oil"*. (KJV)

If you read this book it talks about a woman who had nothing to eat after her husband had passed on, left her with nothing. Then she asked Elisha to help her in her situation, in this context the woman used what she had which was the oil to gain even more oil because of how she thought, then as small as the oil was it was helpful because she was not scared to offer the small amount of oil she had. In your case just offer what you currently have for your gain as little as you may see it, it can be impacted when you meet the right people. Whatever talent you have please do not hide it because someone somewhere may need someone like you with what you have.

You have all the abilities to be successful. You are a producer of your life, you can be multiplied. You can subdue above everything and have dominion above all that you want to achieve. When you have a successful mind set you understand your abilities as where your strength is. With that kind of mind set you understand that failure is a step to a success not a way of stepping back. With a successful mind set you get a better understanding in learning things and initiate them. What do I mean by saying a **successful mind set** I mean you have a learning, accepting and renewable kind of a mind that is able to agree with a situation, a mind that does not take any opportunity for granted, a mind that is always ready to partake from digesting new things, a mind that is teachable and willing to know better.

Successful people still act and walks by faith. They understand a secret of a good debt and create a good reputation for themselves. When you want to be successful you got to understand and follow principles and take good advices. Another thing that I have learnt from successful people with a productive minds they know that money doesn't make them rich but information and knowledge do. They write their plans for future they don't just do for the sake of money, yes they need money but proper planning is their priority.

DISCOVERING REQUIRES EDUCATION, GROWTH AND MATURITY

As I mentioned earlier that you need information and knowledge that requires you to be well-educated about the industry you are getting into. Grow in it and see growth within the industry. Learn more about it and be matured.

Successful mind is not a poor mind, you cannot think poor if you mean business. You need to always be out there looking for information and be updated about everything. Think smart and think fast. You need to know your strengths and weaknesses and work hard to improve your weaknesses. You must pray for what you desire the most and respond to it by believing in faith.

There are questions you need to ask yourself as that successful person or a *wannabe successful person* questions as:

- What gives me a great joy in all that I want or that I am doing?
- What do you consider it a simple?
- Is your vision legally enough in a sense that it won't affect other people's peace?
- Is this vision.. dream or a talent enough for me to get up and do something about it..?
- It is scaring me enough for me not to rest but get up and do something.

Then if you are not sure about these questions then your mindset is not yet ready to succeed and you are not ready enough to be in the field with successful people.

As ready as you may be just please work your mind through and let it agreed strongly with positive sense.